VALE, E.
A PORTRAIT OF ENGLISH CHU
013226 01   726.5 F

OXFORD BROOKES UNIV

This book is

Books m.

D1429546

A Portrait of
ENGLISH CHURCHES

Weston Zoyland, Somerset. The church has one of the finest and most lofty towers in the county. Victims of the Monmouth Rebellion were herded in here for safe-keeping after the Battle of Sedgemoor (1685)

A Portrait of

ENGLISH CHURCHES

A Selection of Photographs by

A. F. KERSTING, F.R.P.S.

with text by

EDMUND VALE

London

B. T. BATSFORD LTD

First published, 1956

PRINTED AND BOUND IN GREAT BRITAIN
BY JARROLD AND SONS LTD, LONDON AND NORWICH
FOR THE PUBLISHERS
B. T. BATSFORD LTD
4 FITZHARDINGE STREET, PORTMAN SQUARE
LONDON, W. I

CONTENTS

AUTHOR'S NOTE

I HAVE always strictly observed the rule never to write about any place or thing I have not seen for myself without warning the reader, as nothing can ever take the place of the personal impression. But with regard to the captions of the illustrations (printed in italic type) I must add a note of warning! The publishers (who are well known for their skill in this matter) first selected the pictures and, in a few cases, I have been able to follow them in the spirit only and not the body, relying on the eyes and judgments of other writers to make comment. So I hope if any fault is found at any point my critic will write to me c/o the Publishers and point it out.

Summer, 1956   E.V.

Figure of the Risen Christ, with crown of thorns and stigmata, on the tower of Fairford church, Gloucestershire—a survival of the earlier church

*Tiverton, Devon. The parish church. The large chantry chapel
was erected by the wool-merchant, John Greenway, in 1517*

St. Mary-the-Virgin, Oxford. The University church, with Early English tower, Decorated spire, Perpendicular nave, and Renaissance porch

THE ENGLISH PARISH CHURCH

No previous age has ever been so acutely conscious of the opposite values of time-present and time-past as our own. While the explorers of science present us with new sources of power, new turns of speed, and new basic raw materials at a rate that makes all earlier "marches of progress" seem funereal, the archaeologist unravels mysteries of the past with a vigour and at a pace almost as astonishing. At the same time, bodies interested in the preservation of bygones spend infinite pains and money in caring for them and forestalling their decay. It is almost as if Nature were working to allay the fevers of nuclear fission by a sedative induced through the contemplation of ancient monuments. In this respect, collectively speaking, no group of ancient monuments has a greater claim on our regard than our parish churches.

Under the authority of the Ancient Monuments Act of 1913 considerable public funds are spent in arresting further decay in far-gone ruins of the Middle Ages—castles and monasteries, whose day was long since spent. These venerable remnants, partly because of their official adoption, partly because of their comparative rarity and, not least perhaps, because you have to buy a ticket to see over them, attract more visitors than the ordinary village church, which suffers the psychological drawbacks of being ubiquitous and free of entry. And it may be noted that, in spite of this building being part of the State "establishment", the Government does next to nothing to help with repairs and the upkeep of the fabric, funds for which must still come from parishioners and the wider public as the result of appeals.

Yet it is surely no small thing that the parish church is a whole building and not a ruin, that it is *not* an outmoded but a living institution, that in most instances its threshold has been trodden by every generation since the village was a village—often a time and circumstance already lost to memory when Domesday Book was compiled. Indeed the first hallowing of that sacred spot may have been a pagan rite performed a thousand years before the birth of Christ, its sanctity confirmed with a new consecration by some early missioner. Certainly no other building can claim such a long unbroken chain of association with human affairs, touching so many lives from birth to death, as the parish church. Nowhere else can be found such an ample museum of record (where real things are seen in the places to which they have always belonged), speaking direct to eye and heart of every change in taste, fashion, outlook, and slant of thought of succeeding generations throughout our national history.

The subject is a voluminous one. Here it will only be attempted to give a general visual impression of the variety of our parish churches, their parts, their structural evolution, and the mementoes they contain of well-being and of stress, of religious conflict, and of souls departed.

Fairfield Church on Romney Marsh, Kent, dedicated to St. Thomas-à-Becket

Ewelme, Oxfordshire. Church and almshouses. The latter, a free school, and the nave and chancel of the church were built by William de la Pole, 1st Duke of Suffolk, in the first half of the fifteenth century. Within, the chantry tomb of the Duchess (nèe Alice Chaucer, believed to be grand-daughter of the poet) is the most intact and perhaps the finest in any parish church. The extraordinary story of the Duke's political murder at sea is fully reported in the Paston Letters (Letter xxvii)

Brading, Isle of Wight. The parish church, looking west out of the Oglander chapel

The canvasses in lozenge-shaped frames were hatchments, a type of memorial that succeeded the placing of personal armour on a tomb. The custom was to display a hatchment on the house of the deceased for some six months after his demise, and then hang it over his tomb or the family vault in the church. Hatchments followed the ordinary rules of heraldry, but they take the story one step further, for they tell not only of the dead but the existence of a survivor as well. This is shown by making one half of the background white—if the sinister side of the shield (the observer's right) is white a widow survives, reversely, a widower. If all is black it is for a bachelor or the last partner in matrimony

Winchelsea, Sussex. One of the Ancient Towns affiliated to the Cinque Ports. Of the large parish church only the chancel remains—a fine example of the Decorated style

Hornchurch, Essex. The stone head of a bull with copper horns is a most unusual feature—a rebus of the place-name, or is it the other way round? The present building is mainly fifteenth-century but its predecessor does seem to have given the place its name which, in the thirteenth century, was written "Hornedchurch"

Capel-y-Ffin, a chapel of ease in the heart of the Black Mountains, Wales

ARCHITECTURAL LINEAGE

WHAT, you might ask, at the outset, is a parish? The name means the district surrounding the church, from which one may infer that the first churches were established before the first parish boundaries were drawn. That would take us back to the fourth century at least, when Britain was still a province of the Roman Empire. And we have a single surviving relic from about that time in the shape of the foundations of a stone-built church at Silchester, one of the model towns established by the conquerors with the intention of making the Britons conform to the Roman way of life—the commercial and administrative centre of the Tribe *Atrebates*. This Christian church was a small affair compared with other places of worship in the town dedicated to Roman and Celtic deities, and it would no doubt have been a matter of great satisfaction to the handful

of devotees forming its congregation to have known that after a lapse of sixteen hundred years their descendants could still find a church to attend at Silchester (one of the only two buildings now to be seen, the other a farm, standing on the grass-covered hundred acres contained within the ruined town wall), though not a single temple dedicated to the old gods could be found in the whole of Britain.

But there was a wide gap in consecutive history between the old ruin (concealed under the greensward until the excavation of 1892) and the newer church, a quarter of a mile away, which has nothing to show in its fabric earlier than the twelfth century, where a stout Norman pillar marks the coming of another conqueror. Christianity had indeed taken firm enough root to survive the departure of the Roman legions. The Church in Britain, cut off from all contact with any other except that in Gaul, became independent and wholly national. But the Britons were roughly handled by the pagan Angles and Saxons and, east of the mountain barrier of Wales, the sites of the many churches they must have dedicated have nearly all been lost to memory. When Augustine came to Kent in the last year but three of the sixth century on his mission from Rome (addressed solely to the Anglo-Saxons, not the Britons), it is on record that he found two churches of the earlier days of Imperial occupation remaining in Canterbury; one in sufficient repair to be used by King Ethelbert's Christian Queen, Bertha, the other fallen into ruin, but repaired and enlarged by him for his cathedral.

There followed a dual march of conversion. From the south, Augustine and his successors spread the Latin usage with subjection to the papal court in Rome while, from the north, missioners from Iona were making striking conversions among the Northumbrians according to the observance of the ancient British Church. But it was the Latin way which emerged triumphant from the Synod of Whitby in 664, and Saxon England became Roman Catholic, the native Church shrinking back to the Celtic fringe. Between the fifth and seventh centuries the structures of the British Church had been homely affairs of wood and wattle but the Saxons, now in regular contact with Rome, were more ambitious and "architectural". They

Wissington, Suffolk. A Norman church with apsidal chancel

Milford-on-Sea, Hampshire. A Norman church lengthened westward in the thirteenth century by addition of the tower and unusual lean-to aisles, now dwarfed by later reconstructions

St. Levan, Cornwall. A typical Cornish church in granite with bold, simple features and separately-roofed nave and aisles

made churches in mortared stone and (re-used) Roman brick—the first to be so built in Britain since the evacuation of the Legions. No doubt many of these interesting buildings would have survived in whole or in part if it had not been for another irruption of pagan invaders in the shape of the Danes who destroyed nearly every Christian building, church or monastery, in the lands they succeeded in gaining and holding, and those through which they marched in armed strength. So that very little indeed remains of that *first period* of Anglo-Saxon architecture which lasted from the seventh to the ninth century.

There was practically no rebuilding for a

hundred years, when a tremendous revival set in, in the latter part of the tenth century, under King Edgar and Archbishop Dunstan. It is to this *second period* that most of the Anglo-Saxon work in our parish churches belongs. Its leading features are noted and illustrated on pages 23–25. It is so crude as to suggest that the Saxons were incapable of fine art, yet much of their carved work on stone and nearly all their manuscript illumination is quite the reverse.

It is only in the parish churches and their ancient burial grounds that any Saxon work remains at all. Nothing is left in any cathedral or monastery of pre-Conquest date. The Normans made no attempt to repair, restore, or enlarge these more important buildings, they simply pulled them down and erected purely Norman structures in their place. To use a colloquialism, particularly apt in this context, the Normans were "funny" about Saxon work. They replaced it wherever funds and labour permitted, and even went to the extent of concealing finely carved stone panels by using them as common building material in walls. It is not always remembered that these people were heathen Vikings a century earlier, that their Christianity, and their adopted Frankish culture and language was barely three generations deep. Though wonderfully adaptable as well as ambitious, they developed their architectural style (based on the far-flung ruins of Imperial Rome) as a sort of major operation, safeguarded by a fixed range of conventions and decorated with repeats of a few stereotyped ornaments. The extent of their achievement in building, rebuilding, or altering several thousand parish churches within the twelfth century is simply astonishing, apart from their vast undertakings in cathedrals and monasteries at the same time. Examples of Norman Romanesque are shown and annotated on pages 27–29. The style may suggest a formal and regimented piety, but it has a way with it of making an appeal which its would-be imitators in the nineteenth century were never able to catch. The tiniest village church with a Norman door or chancel-arch is rendered a solemn and impressive building.

Bamburgh, Northumberland. The church is one of the largest and most interesting in the county. It is dedicated to St. Aidan and stands on the site of his oratory (seventh century)

Finchingfield, Essex. A fine parish church in flint, with work of many periods. Here, one sees a Norman west door, a window of the four-teenth-century aisle, a Perpendicular clerestory and belfry lights. The Renaissance cupola replaces a spire blown down in 1658

ROMANESQUE AND GOTHIC

THE Saxons had also either based their architectural forms on those of ancient Rome or (second period) those of Charlemagne, who had copied from the same source. So there was a kinship of school between their Romanesque and that of the Normans. But before the end of the twelfth century a completely new system of building appeared, distinguished from the other by the name (given at a much later date) of Gothic. In it the arch, instead of being round-headed was pointed, an alteration which had a profound structural effect on the whole building. Primarily, it solved an old vexed question of how to construct a stone ceiling (*vault*) over the nave and choir of a great church and thereby minimise the all-prevalent risk of fire. This could be done without much difficulty in the narrower spaces of the aisles by cross-groining but, for the greater breadth of the main body of the building, the semi-circular arch imposes strict limitations which are overcome by the pointed, or elliptical, arch. In England this discovery appears to have been first exploited with all its advantages at Wells, when the cathedral was being rebuilt in 1174. In consequence of this pointed vaulting of the ceilings, both of the clerestory and the aisles, it was naturally better to point the heads of the window openings at both those stages to fit in with the groining, rather than to stick conservatively to the semi-circular shape. And, as the pointed arch was found pleasing, it was repeated everywhere, in all openings, quite irrespective of structural needs. By the beginning of the thirteenth century the pointed opening was an architectural fashion which had no longer any connection with the manner in which a building was roofed. Parish churches (which hardly ever aspired to the luxury of a stone roof) had all newly made doors, windows, arcades, chancel and tower arches, pointed. The fashion prevailed no less in castles and domestic buildings.

But the pointed opening was not by any means the only feature of the Gothic revolution. For the greater churches, where the new stone roofs had been installed, the flying buttress was invented to counter the outward thrust of the weighty ceiling. The parish church with its wooden roofs had no need for these majestic props but, in the new mode, the true function of the buttress had come into its own for the first time. Wooden roofs, though not exerting the prevailing thrust of stone ones, tend to spread, and the Normans had played for safety in all cases by building extra thick walls. Their buttresses were mere flat pilasters which seem to have been intended for ornament rather than utility. The new walls were built of normal thickness and their stability assured by buttresses of deep projection which gave real support.

Triangular-headed Saxon doorway at Holy Trinity Church, Colchester, Essex, worked in re-used brick from the ruined Roman town

Furthermore, the whole system of decoration was revised. Instead of a repetition of one of the old standard ornaments—chevron, billet, or beak-head—applied to the wall-face round openings, the openings themselves were worked into a series of ridges and hollows, *linear mouldings*, whose function was to give an appearance of grace and lightness to the arch, a note that was also emphasised in the piers of the arcade, where the stout Norman pillar was replaced by one more slender, or lightened in appearance by a cluster of shafts. At the junction between pier and arch the elephantine ponderousness of capitals in the Norman manner was replaced by deeply carved foliage, conventional but spirited. Beyond this last, the only regular ornament (as opposed to moulding) was a small dissected pyramid, now usually referred to as "dog-tooth". Typologists, who never feel happy about the spontaneous generation of ideas, derive this ornament from the Norman nail-head. That may or may not be the case. In its Gothic form it was a brilliant novelty and such an essential feature of the first stage of the new architecture that, wherever found, it is a reliable dating-clue to that stage, for it vanishes for ever as soon as the second development sets in.

Brixworth, Northamptonshire. Early Saxon church constructed of re-used Roman brick. It is basilican in plan but the aisles have been demolished; the door and lower windows are set in blocked arches of the nave arcades

Earl's Barton, Northamptonshire. The tower is late Saxon with pilaster-strips, long-and-short work at the angles, and lathe-turned balusters

Porticus *of the late Saxon church at Bradford-on-Avon, Wiltshire*

Cambridge. Church of the Holy Sepulchre, modelled on the church of that name at Jerusalem (but nothing to do with the Knights Templars). The round nave is early twelfth century, the rectangular chancel fifteenth. It was heavily restored by the Camden Society in 1841. The interior (below) shows the arrangement of the circular aisled nave and clerestory. Compare with Norman representation of the Jerusalem prototype on the Lenton font, page 73

Elkstone, Gloucestershire. A small Norman church in the Cotswolds with stone-vaulted chancel and square-ended sanctuary, each separated by a decorated arch of two orders. The hood-mould over the chancel arch has the pellet ornament, the sanctuary arch, the billet

Although our ancient cities had a great cathedral in their midst they also had numerous parish churches within the confined space of their walls. St. Mary-Arches at Exeter is fully aisled and retains its Norman arcades

Kilpeck, Herefordshire. This small and perfect Norman church (aisleless and with rounded apse) is enriched with carving, within and without, of exceptional verve and quality suggesting Scandinavian or Irish influence. But the craftsman must have had a touch of individual genius and an extraordinary sense of fun to have adapted so many traditional fixations out of the solemn old Norman pattern book and breathed new life and meaning into them. The carving would be unique but for another example at Shobden in the same county—clearly by the same hand. Left : Detail of doorway showing an armed man wearing nether garments reminiscent of modern trousers supported by a girdle

New Romney, Kent. One of the Cinque Ports. But the sea has retreated over a mile and the place has shrunk to the size of a small village. Still it has a mayor. His election takes place round a tomb in the parish church (here seen) *whose fine Norman tower shows the break to Transitional work in its uppermost stage*

ERRATA

Page 29. The caption to the top illustration on this page should read *Bishopstone, Sussex. The Chancel Arch.*

The lower photograph is of *New Romney, Kent. Chipstead, Surrey* is illustrated on page 30.

Chipstead, Surrey. Small lancet lights, Early English style, rabbeted (probably) *to receive wooden frames holding oiled linen instead of glass*

Chipstead, Surrey. Early English lancet windows in the North Transept

THE GOTHIC STYLES

IT was shown early in the nineteenth century by Thomas Rickman that the Gothic art of building could be divided into three main stages and three sub-stages, a feat of analysis which gave the Romantic movement the ballast it had sorely lacked since it had first ventured forth into uncharted seas of imaginative frenzy a century earlier. Rickman's classification still holds good and may be said to cover a space of time from the late twelfth century, when the rebuilding of Wells Cathedral was begun, to the early sixteenth when, so to speak, the two big R's were in the air—Reformation and Renaissance. The three *styles*, as Rickman called those stages of evolution, he named Early English, Decorated, and Perpendicular, the sub-stages, Transitional (from Norman to Early English), and Early and Late Decorated, otherwise known by the more descriptive terms of Geometric and Flamboyant.

The most remarkable features of this Gothic progression were, first, the universal acceptance of each step-up in the art as it occurred, remote places in far-off corners of the land copying the new mode meticulously within a few years after the fashion had set in and abandoning the old and, secondly, the consistency with which each "style" was maintained throughout a long period till the next "came in", with only slight variations, all duly reflected throughout the country.

There is not the space here to explain all the points of each style but a general idea will be gained from the illustrations showing typical examples, and notes appended to them, and from the following summary. Stage 1 we have already spoken of and mentioned that it may be dated from 1174 with the re-edification of Wells Cathedral. It then emerged as a full-blown style though the change had been heralded by various signs a little earlier (Rickman's "Transitional") and the amenity of the pointed arch in vaulting had been discovered in France and imported by the Cistercians into Yorkshire and Shropshire in the fifties—it could be maintained that Durham made an independent discovery still earlier. Credit for the change to Decorated is probably

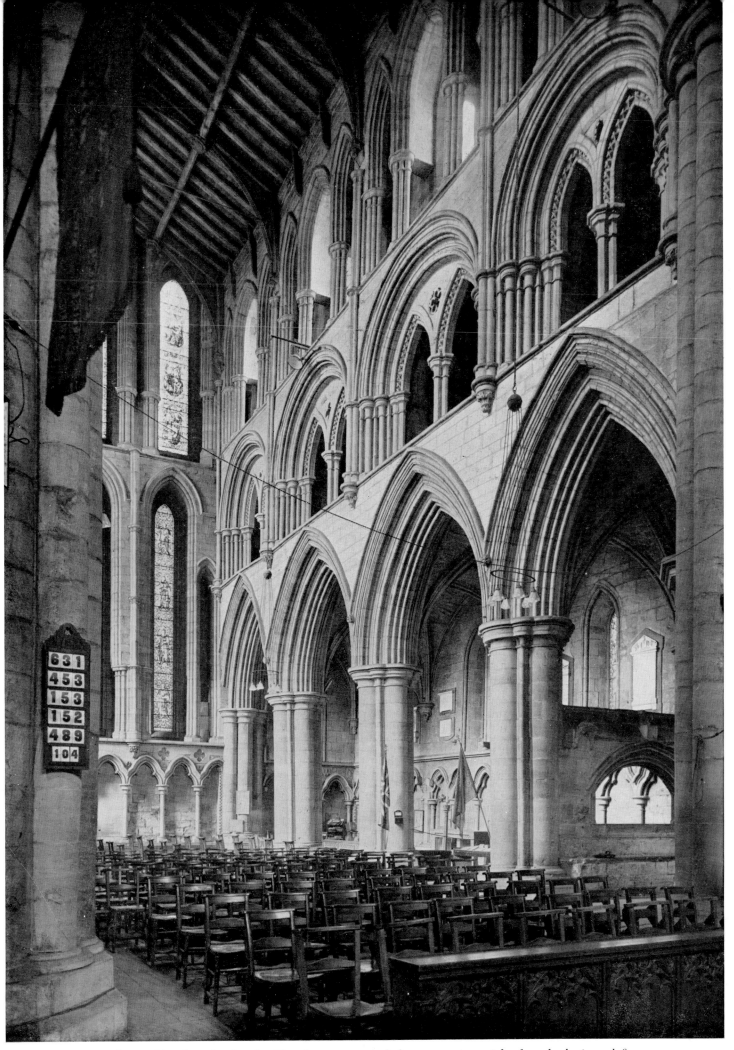

Hexham, Northumberland. North transept of the present parish church designed for the more elaborate requirements of an Augustinian priory. The work is mid-thirteenth century and an admirable example of the fully developed Early English style

due to the designer of the Angel choir at Lincoln. This is said to have been put in hand about 1256, but attention would hardly be drawn to it before the great ceremony of 1280, when the body of St. Hugh was translated to the new shrine there prepared, in the presence of King Edward I. Yet just about that year, or very shortly after, the new parish church of Acton Burnell in Shropshire was completed, a perfect little model, bearing all the authentic marks of the Decorated style.

It could be objected that such a quick echo from far-off Lincoln was an exceptional rather than a typical case, for the builder, Robert Burnell, Bishop of Bath and Wells, was King Edward's chancellor and might well know what had been going on at Lincoln for the past score of years. At all events, before the end of that century, parish churches in many different parts of the country were carrying out new work in the Early Decorated style.

The principal achievement of this Stage 2 was the development of the compound window from the simple one-light lancet form of its predecessor. By the introduction of stone supports for the glass—mullions in the lower part and tracery in the head—the width of windows was greatly increased and more light admitted. To begin with, the tracery which filled the head of the window had the somewhat heavy effect of a stone grid and was designed in purely geometrical patterns, on which account the ugly but descriptive sub-stage name of "geometric" was given. But quite early in the fourteenth century this rigid formula had given place to tracery in which the bars of stone were much reduced in heaviness and took the form of harmonic curves balanced on either side of the head, an improvement distinguished by the name "flowing".

The flowing tracery of this period is one of the greatest charms of the style and one of its highest artistic achievements. To us, its silhouette remains a thing of beauty, but the pictures in coloured glass it was primarily designed to frame in a rhythmic conception made it a double joy, as may be seen by the few examples which survived the deliberate smashings of the sixteenth and seventeenth

Godalming, Surrey. East window of South Chapel in the parish church: Early Decorated; geometric tracery with pierced cusps. The doorway below, a post Reformation insertion after the removal of the altar which the window was intended to light

centuries. As already said, the dog-tooth ornament disappeared as soon as the Early English style went out of date. It vanished with an extraordinary suddenness and precision in the last quarter of the thirteenth century, its place being taken by what is called the "ball-flower". This was of the same size and fulfilled the same purpose as the discredited dog-tooth. It could be used singly, in small groups, or repeated in close formation along the line of a hollow moulding, giving a window-frame, for instance, a lively garlanded look. The ball-flower may have been first inspired from the cracked husk of a horse-chestnut showing the polished fruit between its four points, or from the yellow water-lily. But it was, and always remained, as conventional as anything achieved by the Early English carver. Yet in all other decoration, on capitals, on canopies, in spandrels, the works of Nature were not represented conventionally, as the Early English carver had done with his "stiff leaf foliage", but *naturally*. This was part and parcel of the luxuriance of the style and is generally much admired for the verisimilitude of its oak-leaves and acorns, its maple foliage, and flowering herb-Bennet. Yet these true-to-life copies, no matter how cleverly wrought, lack the challenging force of the more ascetic inventions of the first pioneers of Gothic. Everywhere, enrichment was added to enrichment till the year 1349 was rung in, when the grisly hand of the Black Death halted the Decorated style.

For the whole of the remaining half of that century very little new building work was carried out, and work already in progress was left unfinished for a long period, for the plague had reduced and disorganised the labour force and increased building costs. In this interim a gradual change was taking place which, shortly before the year 1400, had fully developed into the last of the Gothic styles, to which Rickman's name "Perpendicular" still adheres. The change appears to have sprung from one particular and definite source, namely, the Abbey of Gloucester, where the monks were engaged in converting the dark Norman choir of their church (now Gloucester Cathedral) into a presbytery that should be not only well

A well-balanced design in flowing tracery —late Decorated—in the north transept of Huish Episcopi church, Somerset. It is the reversal of so many curves which gives the effect of "flow" and, for instance, creates the illusion that the quatrefoil in the top window has "sprouted out" of the head of the middle light in the lower part

Woolpit, Suffolk. The church has one of the finest porches (with room over) in East Anglia. It is decorated with knapped flint and freestone flushwork and was added in the fifteenth century to an aisle a century older

Sleaford, Lincolnshire. The church has one of the earliest broach spires (first quarter of the thirteenth century). The large windows of the aisle are mid-fourteenth century and show well the flamboyant tracery of the Late Decorated style

lit but well able to display a wealth of the improved stained glass. This renovation was actually going on at the time of the Black Death and the work was able to continue uninterrupted, for Gloucester was one of the few lucky places which escaped the great plague.

The name "Perpendicular" was given on account of one of the most obvious features of the new style which one can detect at a glance. In windows, the mullions no longer break off at the spring of the arch to fill the head with curving lines of flowing tracery, they persist as perpendicular bars from the sill to the point where they meet the arch. The structural reason for this is that the windows are now made as large in area as possible both by broadening them between jambs and, at the same time, gaining more space in the head by flattening out the arch which, instead of being struck from two centres, as heretofore, is struck from four. This means that the tracery itself has to bear some of the weight of the wall above without wholly relying on the arch to do so,

and the perpendicular mullions provide that reinforcement.

The four-centred arch is as much a mark of the style as the sill-to-arch mullion. Its use in the nave arcade, by increasing the height from the floor to the spring of the arch, gave more space between the columns, letting in more light to the middle of the church. Before the end of the fourteenth century fresh work in parish churches reflected the new mode, which had reached almost full maturity by the early years of the fifteenth century.

In decoration, the Perpendicular style was not marked by a single characteristic emblem like the dog-tooth and the ball-flower. Partly from the necessity of economising in costs, and partly the greater mastery of engineering efficiency gained after two centuries of Gothic construction, there was a general simplification. The window tracery was far less complicated; it was more useful as a grating for the display of glass than a thing of beauty in itself. The mouldings, with their complex groups of ribs

Fairford, Gloucestershire. One of the last churches to be rebuilt before the Reformation (consecrated 1493). It shows the full development of the Perpendicular style and is famous for its contemporary stained glass (page 81)

35

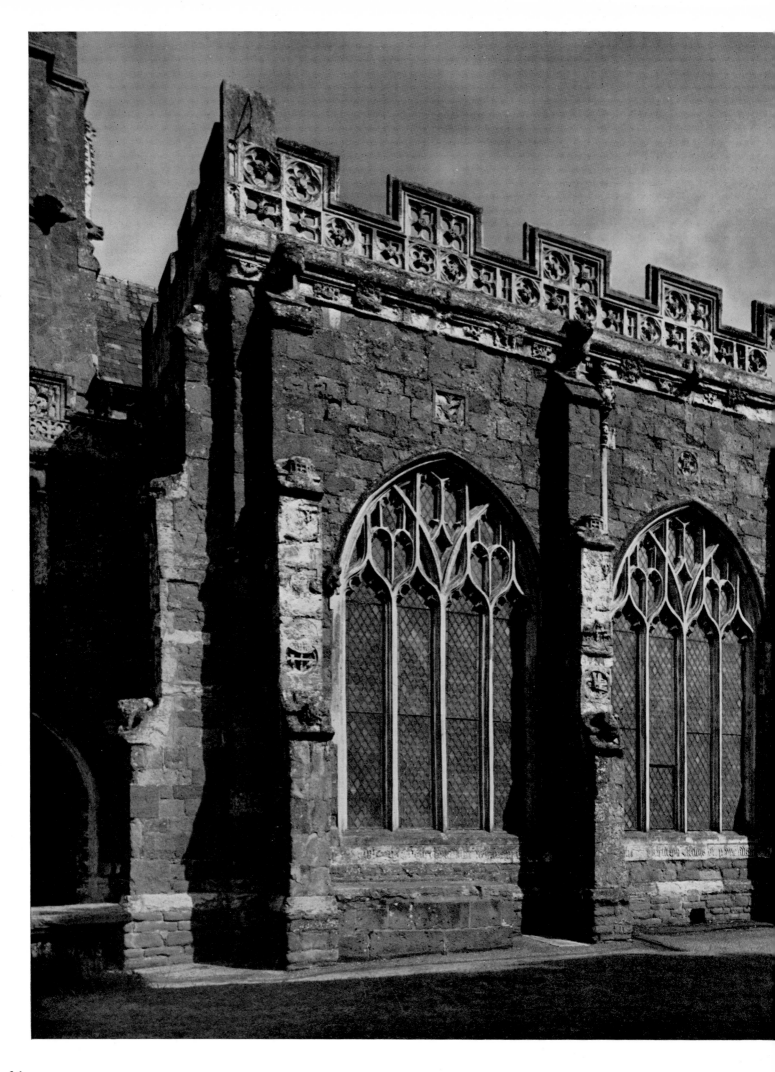

Cullompton, Devon. Additional south aisle built in 1528 by the merchant, John Lane. His merchant's mark and ships carrying his ventures are carved on the buttresses

and hollows, were reduced to the simplest terms, the most characteristic being the *casement* mould which was a single hollow swept into a half undulation. In fact, there was a tendency for mechanical proficiency to express itself to the exclusion of art and individuality. But, whatever the earlier styles had owed to derived forms from the Continent, Perpendicular was an all-English invention, its triumphs and its higher achievements (like King's College Chapel, Cambridge) were native expressions of art and engineering. It was the last word in the evolution of Gothic—and we were the only folk privileged to speak it!

Though the choir and Lady Chapel of Gloucester Abbey and the chapter-house and two-decker cloister of Old St. Paul's[1] were the pioneers of Perpendicular, and Winchester Cathedral and Sherborne Abbey converted their Norman naves ("all standing", as the sailors say) to that style, and the nave of Canterbury was rebuilt in it, it is not in the greater church but the parish church that it can be best seen in every phase and local idiom and in every quarter of the kingdom.

[1] Destroyed in the Great Fire of London, 1666.

The fifteenth century saw the ravages of the Black Death repaired, population on the increase, and trade, particularly in the several centres of the woollen and clothing industries, flourishing, in spite of the Wars of the Roses. At the same time, a renewed intensity of religious fervour turned the attention of parishioners to thoughts of restoration. Their long neglected churches were much decayed and generally inadequate. More room in them was needed, and they must have seemed both ritually and architecturally out of date. Smaller and poorer parishes had to be content with adding a new aisle but, where funds were available, the great desire was to have (as well) a clerestory added to the nave. In earlier days only the greater churches had this amenity. For them, it was part of the traditional three-stage arrangement of the time-honoured basilican plan—an aisled building, surmounted by triforium and then clerestory. But the wish of townsmen and villagers to have this top-lighting in their churches was not just emulation of the cathedral style but to give fuller expression to the cult of the rood-loft which had grown to a greatly

Lavenham, Suffolk. This church was rebuilt (except for the chancel) between 1485 and 1525 by the rich clothier, Thomas Spring, and John de Vere, Earl of Oxford, many lesser folk also subscribing

Cromer, Norfolk. This finely proportioned building is one of the most dignified of our parish churches in the Perpendicular style. The square window with pierced tracery in the ringing-chamber is a striking local feature of the Norfolk towers

Burwell, Cambridgeshire. Following a prayer for the founders (or rebuilders) on the carved panel over the chancel arch, the date of the building is given as 1464. The interior stonework is local clunch

increased popularity. The addition of a clerestory not only provided better lighting for the intricately carved and coloured woodwork of the new screens and the three great figures poised above the loft (the Crucifix, with the Virgin and St. John on either hand), it gave a greater height for these to be displayed above the chancel-arch, an additional space that could be further used for the painting of a doom-picture.

The majority of parish churches carried out these improvements in the nave while leaving as much of the extant fabric as intact as possible. In some cases the clerestory was the only addition, an enlarged floor-space either not being required or sacrificed to pay for the clerestory. But, in many instances, the bolder decision was reached to pull down the old nave and rebuild with all the latest appurtenances, leaving chancel and tower as they were, or, again, including one, or rebuilding all three.

The effect of the part-alteration is often a sin against symmetry and proportion but, with other accretions, governed by accident rather than taste, it is one of those things which contributes to the charm and interest of the building and adds to its venerableness if not its beauty. And it must be borne in mind that the nave (with tower and porches) and their necessary repairs or reconstruction were regarded as the responsibility of the parish, while the chancel and all appertaining to it was the affair of the Church. This division of powers was marked by the wall separating the two, pierced by the chancel-arch which was, in effect, a party-wall and, on that account, often remained unaltered, though more than one rebuilding (as clerks or parishioners had found means to keep step with fashion) had taken place on either side. It is owing to this uncertainty as to who should pay for alterations in the party-wall that we are happy in retaining so many more Norman chancel-arches and others of earlier date than the compartments they separate.

The parish church, Long Melford, Suffolk, with its unique Lady chapel situated east of the main building, as in a cathedral. All except the tower is late fifteenth century

St. James's, Piccadilly, London: by Wren, in the new fashionable quarter rapidly developing after the Great Fire. Completed, 1684. Restored 1953 by Professor Sir Albert Richardson after war damage

RENAISSANCE

IT must be reckoned one of the strangest coincidences of history that the Renaissance Movement should reach England so near the time of the Reformation that Protestantism and the neo-classical type of church seem inseparably linked. But Renaissance had already killed Gothic before the official era of Protestantism set in. Even if the old allegiance to Rome and the manner of its observances had continued unchanged, it seems unlikely that the Gothic tradition would have had a further lease of life. Henry VIII, while still defender of the old faith, had definitely become a patron of the Italianate fashion. There is an almost startlingly graphic illustration of this in the chapel of King's College, Cambridge.

This great building was only completed in 1515 (as to the stonework), when the fan-vaulted ceiling was finished, a culminating feat of art and engineering that was the finest flower of the three centuries of Gothic evolution. After that, the glazing of the windows went forward, then came the wooden furnishings. Of these, the first to be erected was the rood-loft. King Henry presented it to his royal college. It was of cathedral dimensions with a depth of nine feet between the eastern and western screens, the loft above being fifteen feet wide. But the design is pure Renaissance without the least trace of Gothic influence. It must have been erected in or shortly after the year 1531, for it bears in one compartment the arms of Anne Boleyn and, in another, her initial, linked with that of her perfidious husband by a true lover's knot. Henry was then a Roman Catholic and a

Berwick-upon-Tweed, Northumberland. One of the few churches to be built during the Commonwealth, it was erected by Colonel Fenwick, Governor of the town, in 1652. Classical, but blended with much Gothic feeling

St. Mary's, Warwick. A parish church formerly served by a college of priests. A fire in 1694 destroyed the nave and tower, though the medieval choir and chapels at the east end escaped owing to their stone screens and vaulted roofs. Nave and tower were rebuilt four years later, Sir William Wilson being in charge of the work. Wren was consulted and fee'd for designs but it remains uncertain how much of the accomplished work is Wren and how much Wilson. The result is a sort of topical compromise between Gothic and Renaissance

West Wycombe, Buckinghamshire. The parish church, rebuilt in the eighteenth century on the site of a Norman predecessor under the patronage of Sir Francis Dashwood, founder of the Dilettanti Society and the Knights of St. Francis of Wycombe, better known as the Hell Fire Club. The large globe (which can be entered from the belfry) takes the place of a spire and is associated with many unfounded tales of the Club's activities

spiritual vassal of the Pope. By the winter of 1535 he had created himself Supreme Head of the Church of England, endorsed by Parliament under the Act of Supremacy, and the rood was never placed on the loft in King's Chapel—only the organ.

The Reformation naturally acted as a check to the kind of munificence which had been regularly forthcoming to build or rebuild churches for, when prayers for the dead were ruled out, much of the force which had animated zeal and motive was gone, and it was nearly a hundred years before any new churches were built. In the meantime, Renaissance varieties were well established as correct architectural forms for the Protestant Church. It was, as just said, quite a coincidence that things should have taken this turn, but it must have seemed natural enough, for the Reformers had banned all

St. Martin-in-the-Fields (left) and St. Mary-le-Strand (below) are both London churches by James Gibbs whose other best known works are the Radcliffe Camera at Oxford and the Senate House at Cambridge. Though the Italianate manner was in high fashion, Gibbs was almost the only architect of his time who had a close acquaintance with that source, having been pupil to Carlo Fontana, the papal architect, in Rome. In 1713 he was made Surveyor to the Commission charged by Queen Anne to undertake the building of fifty new churches in London. St. Mary-le-Strand was the first of these (begun, 1714) and also Gibbs's first public building. A change of government dislodged him from his official post or we should doubtless have had many more Gibbs churches in London. He undertook St. Martin's in 1722

things made in the likeness of saints and angels, and, in this, Gothic stood condemned and had been physically punished for its error with a million hammer-blows. But heroes of the Old Testament were permitted, and the sombre forms of neo-classicism, which quenched all tendency to superstition, made them seem as sabbatical as the Geneva gown.

A few churches were built in the reign of Charles I, but the great programmes of building and rebuilding did not begin until after the Restoration (1660) when the damages of the Civil War began to be counted, and then after the Great Fire (1666), when the activities of Wren in the City of London gave a new stimulus to church-building in general. In a few places some conservative elements were still able to reproduce the Gothic manner or a near echo of it. One of the most remarkable examples was Charles Church at Plymouth (dedicated to the uncanonised martyr) which was actually built during the Commonwealth but most unfortunately wrecked in the Second World War.

All our Renaissance buildings, whether based on Palladian or Wrennian forms, or the local hybrid called Jacobean, were essentially a return to the manner of Ancient Rome until nearly the end of the eighteenth century, when the two artist travellers, Stuart and Revett, rediscovered the earlier fount of Ancient Greece. Though belated, it made something of a stir, mainly reverberating in the sphere of domestic architecture, but the revival of medieval ideas was already preparing to give Gothic a come-back. This it succeeded in doing most thoroughly by the middle of the nineteenth century—yet there was a certain something that the medieval craftsman had which never came back.

This, in brief, is the story of the architectural lineage of the English parish church, and a very large number of the older buildings can show most of those materially symbolic signs of the times through which they have passed, features which, at a glance, can be identified with one or other period of history. But, while book-history merely relates of the past in current print, the carved stones bear contemporary witness to it, for they received the shapes we can see and touch from the hands of men then alive. The chain which holds our imagination is one which, if uneven, has never snapped. Through the storm of the Reformation and the anti-episcopal régime of the Commonwealth continuity of religious observance persisted; the building remained *in use*.

Worcester. All Saints Church (1738) thought to have been built from designs by Thomas White the Worcester architect. A stand for the city regalia (when the mayor comes to church) is seen in left foreground

Brighton, Sussex. St. Peter's Church is a particularly instructive example of Gothic Revival. The nave and tower are an early experiment in the art by Charles Barry (1824), whose Houses of Parliament some sixteen years later may be said to have tipped the balance in the Battle of the Styles in favour of neo-Gothic. Barry's work here may be described as a sort of free-lance Perpendicular tinged with Georgian hollowness. There was no chancel, as that feature was still regarded as quite un-Protestant and omitted in every new church built at that time. Barry merely supplied a polygonal apse for the holy table. The change of ideas both in Gothic Revival and religious observance are illustrated by the deep chancel now demanded, and here added in 1900 by Somers Clarke with faultless Perpendicular detail tinged with Victorian rectitude

Burgh Castle, Suffolk. The church is a much patched survival. Even the round tower (its earliest member) has had its battlement made up with red brick. The round tower is a strong local feature of East Anglia where 168 were still standing before the 1939–45 war. They are presumed to have had a defensive origin like the round towers of Ireland and only came into use as bell-towers at a later date. The Irish towers are of ninth and tenth century date and several of the East Anglian ones go back to Saxon times

PRINCIPAL PARTS

IT is a notable paradox that while those few architectural styles ruled successively throughout the country with a rigid uniformity of detail never seen since, the smaller buildings in which they were faithfully reflected—our parish churches—should not, in themselves, have uniformity but variety as their outstanding feature. Therein lies their never-ending charm. Such a mingling of art and accident, such a range of local interpretation of current ideas, so many unrecorded carvings rendered unique by the touch of genius, all magically blended by time into part-and-parcel harmony with natural settings which have become beautiful through the long establishment of those consecrated enclosures.

So there are churches which can be called *handsome* on account of their architectural rectitude, and others *picturesque* because they mix all styles, break all rules, and hide their original plans under a mass of accretions. In general, this same plan is a simple one, providing for a building that is to be in one part a House of God and, in the other, a hall for his worshippers. That is to say, it has not merely been thought of as a "place of worship" but

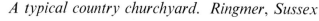

A typical country churchyard. Ringmer, Sussex

Crowhurst, Surrey. The church has a wooden steeple protected by weather-boarding and shingles

Othery, Somerset. A cruciform church with four-light belfry window

Sutton Courtenay, Berkshire. The tower shows Norman, Transitional, and Decorated work in ascending order

also one in which the spirit of the Deity is believed to dwell, a mysterious presence presiding continually at the altar like an invisible host at the high table of his hall. The provision for this mystery is what makes the essential difference between a church and a meeting-house, and this member of the building is called the *chancel*. It is the province of the parish priest and his assistants, and was even more exclusively theirs before the Reformation, when separate access was provided by a *priest's door* on the south side, a feature which has generally been preserved, though sometimes with the opening blocked up. The primary function of the chancel is to give shelter against the weather to the altar, and it was therefore the first part of any new church to be built. But an original chancel is rare, and quite often a

restoration will have replaced it by one more up-to-date, architecturally, than the nave. It is that part of the building which has chief honour, and its enrichments in carved work on wall and roof usually exceed those of the nave. Its boundary was marked (except in the later churches of the fifteenth century) by a structural division in the shape of the *chancel-arch* in that party-wall of joint obligation as to repairs mentioned on page 41.

With the adjoining *nave* the church is "technically" complete, steeple and porch, though rarely missing, being mere accessories after the fact. There have been variations in plan, but the general one adopted in England (called *basilican*, as deriving from the Roman municipal hall) was already foreshadowed in the little fourth-century church at Silchester

Ottery St. Mary, Devon. Dorset aisle with fan-vaulted ceiling, sixteenth century

where the foundations show it to have been a plain rectangle with side aisles and a rounded apse. There is nothing to indicate whether or not it had the upper range of windows (*clerestory*) which properly belonged to the basilica, but this was present in the seventh-century Saxon church at Brixworth as can be seen in the picture on page 24. Later, however (and until the fifteenth century), the clerestory was exceptional in the parish church and the majority, down to the end of the Norman period, were also without aisles, so that the name is misleading except for the greater churches. What they did resemble closely was the hall of the contemporary manor-house. As the population increased, aisles were added (one at a time) to aisleless churches, or widened in those which already possessed them. Early

aisles were narrow so that the unbroken sweep of the roof could cover them. To widen them meant giving them a separate roof under another gable or a lean-to, in which case the walls above the nave arcade must be heightened.

The builders were extremely clever at making these adaptations. They could add one or a pair of aisles to an aisleless nave without causing it to be closed for the daily services. This they did by building the aisles first, then cutting spaces in the existing walls for the insertion of columns to carry the arcades. Next, they would work the arches between the columns, after which the openings could be cleared, leaving the upper part of the old walls standing in air over the new arcades. This process of making do with as much of the old fabric as possible was a handsome contribution to variety in the interior. Thus you may have a late Norman arcade on the north side and an Early English one on the south, while the windows of either aisle may be of any period and not infrequently contain assorted specimens of each.

Such aisles were, in the first instance, installed or added to give more floor-space to a growing congregation whose worship was directed to the single altar in the east of the chancel but, as time went on, more altars were required and found places with correct orientation and good window-lighting against the east walls of the aisles. After the Black Death, in the middle of the fourteenth century, the system of endowing chantries for masses to be said for the departed souls of those who could afford the luxury had become exceedingly popular and prevalent. Such foundations had previously been confined to monastic and cathedral churches, but now space in the parish church was sought to establish these altars and the more easterly bays of the aisles began to be used. The craft guilds also wanted side-chapels; but, whereas it was only necessary to make room for one man—the mass-priest—in a chantry chapel, the ceremonies of the guild would be attended by a goodly company of brethren. This large demand was sometimes met by extending an aisle eastward to lie side by side with the chancel, or by adding yet another

Langford, Oxfordshire. The church (mainly Transitional and Early English) has a central tower but no transepts. It is rich in unusual details, two of which appear in the picture, namely stone figures of the Rood in the gable of the porch and carved canopy gracing the priest's door

Sandwich, the best preserved of all the Cinque Ports, has three parish churches, of which St. Clement's, with its Norman tower enriched by arcading, is the most noble

53

Fingest, Buckinghamshire. The Norman tower is capped by a picturesque double saddle-back roof of uncertain date

Old Malton, Yorkshire. The façade was a feature of monastic and cathedral churches to which the parish church did not aspire, contenting itself with the elaboration of its principal porch; though, after the Reformation, parishes became possessed of churches built for monastic communities, as here. This was the church of a Gilbertine priory (dissolved, 1539). It was converted into a parish church after clerestory, central tower, and both aisles had been pulled down. The façade, once balanced by two western towers, is Early English, including the doorway which, though round-headed, is of the same style in all its detail. The Perpendicular window replaces three lancets, though the jamb-shafts of the outer ones with dog-tooth ornament were left intact, as can be seen

whole aisle, or by throwing out an additional building like the Greenway chantry at Tiverton shown on page 9.

A variation of the basilican plan was the cruciform church in which a transept was built on either side of the nave at right angles to it. This was very popular with the Normans who built many churches on this plan. The transepts, which acted like buttresses to north and south, coupled with the same stability given on the other two sides by nave and chancel, enabled the builders to perch a central tower on four arches at the crossing of the four members of the building. The visual effect of this arrangement from the outside was bold, attractive, and complete. Given the massive treatment of twelfth-century taste it was suggestive of the religious stronghold. But it was more suitable to the monastic and cathedral church which were the first to multiply altars and could use those additional stretches of east-facing wall for the purpose without difficulty, for their transepts were roomy and generally aisled. In the parish church, much of the space gained was wasted, as a view from the transepts towards the chancel with its altar was obscure and the fault only partly remedied by piercing the obstructive angle with a loophole "squint".

It is not certain to what extent the Saxons had followed the basilican plan of terminating the east end with a rounded or polygonal apse but it seems certain that they did not feel bound to do so in every case and often made their chancels square-ended, which appears to have been already an established English prejudice. But the apse was a fixed idea with the Normans, imposed on us willy-nilly as part of the medicine of conquest, though there were indeed a few exceptions. But when the yoke was thrown off in the architectural revolution of the thirteenth century we went back doggedly to the square end, and the apse, in all churches great and small, became as rare as the round-headed arch. In this, as in other insular prejudices, we were not followed on the Continent.

Ault Hucknall, Derbyshire. Its disproportionate late porch and aisle conceal an ancient and interesting interior

PORCH

In addition to the nave and chancel are the steeple and porches. Though ritually not essential to the church they are seldom absent. Their use seems obvious enough—the one to act as a bell-tower to give notice of an impending service, the other to act as a vestibule to the nave. Yet each has a more complex history than either nave or chancel though only a few brief points in their evolution can be given here.

If one goes right back to church building of the seventh century (first Saxon period) one finds the word *porticus* (for porch) used in quite a different sense. A contemporary, writing of the great church built at Hexham by Wilfred, describes it as having "many porches". What these were may be gathered from the now exposed foundations of the seventh-century church at Reculver. Here, the nave and chancel instead of having aisles (in the ordinary sense) are made to communicate through door-like openings with outer chambers, to north, south, and west. Access to the nave was, in fact, by the western *porticus* which was, therefore, to some extent a vestibule. The use of the other "porches" is not quite clear, but a clue to their peculiar sanctity is seen in those which formed part of the Church of St. Peter and St. Paul at Canterbury, founded by St. Augustine, where all the early archbishops, including the founder himself, were entombed.

The church at Bradford-on-Avon (second Saxon period) had a *porticus* on either side of the nave, and that to the north is still intact, as shown in the picture on page 25. Entrance to the church was by either one of these. Yet, as will be observed, each was a large room, something much bigger than what we now understand as a porch. Bradford may be as late as the eleventh century, and in this *porticus* we may perhaps see a transition from the older to the newer use—a kind of side-chapel serving as vestibule. But the chain of evolution is interrupted by the invasion of the Normans who had such definite ideas of their own. In their planning, the *porticus* in its older form must have disappeared some time before they arrived here. Such porches as they built were nothing more than vestibules and they were almost entirely confined to the greater churches. For the parish church they preferred a doorway without any sheltered approach, though distinguished by shafting and carved work which was sometimes more elaborate than anything else about the church.

In the thirteenth century, however, the porch was revived, though now purely as a sheltered approach and in the form familiar to us with side-benches. But it had so much lost its sanctity of character as to be quite a secular

Beccles, Suffolk. The south porch of the parish church. It stands 34 feet high and has a room over with a traceried window looking into the nave. The north porch also has a room over but is plainer

Northleach, Gloucestershire. This porch (mid-fifteenth century), one of the most beautiful in England, retains the original figures in its central niches. The pinnacle on the west side which appears broken is, in fact, a chimney to the fireplace in the upper room which is reached by a stair in the corner turret

The great porch at Cirencester, Gloucestershire, described opposite

appanage to the main body. Coroner's courts were held in it and the first part of the marriage service (embodying the civil contract). It became more and more indispensable for the above-mentioned and other functions as time went on, so that one finds porches of all periods added in front of doorways of earlier date, a thing which has fortunately preserved in freshness many a fine Norman and Early English entrance from weathering.

By the fifteenth century, porches had become little architectural masterpieces with enriched doorways, carved roofs, and stained glass windows. Often they had a dwelling-room over for a priest, sometimes complete with fireplace and other domestic conveniences. The most elaborate and unmistakably secular of all is that of the parish church of Cirencester. It seems to have been the property of the principal craft-guild of the town which had its chapel in the nave of the church. Here, over the stone fan-vaulted porch itself is the hall where the guild held its meetings and feasts, with kitchen, cellar, and room for their chantry priest. After the Reformation this porch became the town hall.

. Mary-the-Virgin, Oxford. The south
rch built by Nicholas Stone in 1637.
e figure of the Virgin, which disappeared
ring the Commonwealth regime, was
covered and replaced later

Pirton, Worcestershire. A unique arrangement whereby a transept and steeple are combined in a single half-timbered erection on the north side of the parish church

extended westward at a later time. That process was not confined to primitive days. The steeple of the great parish church of Grantham stood detached to the west of the building until the fourteenth century when the nave, by a westward extension, not only reached it but overlapped it with its aisles on two sides.

It was natural enough that under Gothic treatment the steeple (with or without a spire) should receive particular attention as to design. It was the most showy part of the church—the sign of the parish, as it were, writ largely in the sky from afar off. So more and more care and thought were given to the disposal of its decorative features, the number and arrangement of belfry windows, the division of the tower into stages by string-courses, the placing of buttresses at the corners, the balance of battlements and pinnacles at the summit. Again, if a spire was added to the tower there

STEEPLE

THE word *steeple* can mean a plain bell-tower or one surmounted by a spire. The latter has no utilitarian function whatever. It is just an ornament pure and simple, made with no other purpose than to strike the imagination. Its invention must be credited to those visionary innovators responsible for the Early English style, as it does not appear before the thirteenth century. The idea originated in the Midlands where some of the most satisfactory spires, proportionable to their towers, may be seen.

The earliest bell-towers of parish churches would seem to have been detached and not part of the building. Some were round and not rectangular; of such there are several pre-Conquest examples in East Anglia. And it can be shown in a few cases that these were originally detached, only becoming part of the body of the church through the nave being

Heckington, Lincolnshire. One of the rare churches all of one plan and time— the middle of the fourteenth century— and one of the most perfect achievements of the Decorated style. The broach spire, whose nature is obscured by parapet and massive pinnacles, is enriched by twelve gabled windows

Huish Episcopi parish church which has one of the most ornate of the Somerset towers

was the eternal question of how to blend the two, besides the geometrical problem of fitting that soaring octagonal figure on to its square substructure. Should the join be made behind the screen of a parapet or in full view, abandoning the parapet—the broach spire? There is no doubt that eventually the steeple became the pride of the parish, especially in Somersetshire. Some kept pace with fashion by wholly rebuilding their bell-towers, others were content to renew the upper parts or add a stage to them. But the steeple was the most economical part of the whole structure. It did not need radical alterations from time to time like the rest of the church and, provided it was well built and roomy enough for a ring of eight bells, it was quite often left alone in its Norman or even Saxon simplicity. In any case, the steeple of the English parish church provides a rich and endless study in variety.

Louth, Lincolnshire. The steeple, 300 feet high, was completed in 1515 and is perhaps the finest tower-with-spire of any parish church in England. The four great turret-like pinnacles are each 50 feet high and act the part of flying buttresses

Saffron Walden, Essex. Belfry and spire by Thomas Rickman, high priest of Gothic Revival. It replaced a wooden spire in 1831 and is a clever adaptation of the East Anglian pinnacle-buttress type but just a thought more Rickmanic than medieval

Castle Cary, Somerset. A steeple of fairly simple but effective design. In the spire, the angles of the octagon are emphasised by roll mouldings and its plain surfaces by a band of carving. The slim pinnacle set diagonally (which is purely ornamental and not functional) and the pierced parapet are made great play with in the Somerset towers of the fifteenth century

Newdigate, Surrey. This wooden shingled spire of pyramidal type caps a weather-boarded belfry containing a ring of eight bells. The whole weight is carried on four oak beams 17 inches square

64

Duntisbourne Rous, Gloucestershire. The tall fourteenth-century churchyard cross is nearly perfect—its head only slightly broken

CHURCHYARD

LASTLY comes the churchyard. But it should not be thought of as "lastly" out of the present context for it must often have existed before the church. A very large number of our present parish churches are successors to those named in Domesday Book. Of them some must have been founded by Saxon thegns, new-built within new enclosures. Others must have occupied sites consecrated by the Early British Church before the Anglo-Saxon invasion. And it is clear that the Britons often founded their churches on ground that had long been held sacred by their pagan forefathers both for worship and burial, for there are churchyards in which prehistoric remains still exist. The presence of yew trees is probably a living link with that dim past.

The origin of the association of the yew tree with the churchyard remains a mystery in spite of all likely guesses and so, to some extent, does that of the churchyard cross. Its presence was particularly abhorrent to the Reformers and only a very few remain intact, though their broken shafts, or bases with the empty sockets in which they stood, abound. These crosses are mainly of post-Conquest date and are much plainer than the earlier series which were elaborately carved with vine-scroll and interlace patterns. Formerly regarded as works of Celtic art those earlier crosses have now been traced to an origin in Northumbria, and the credit given not to the Britons but the Angles.

The subject of the pre-Norman churchyard cross is deep and fascinating, but the story too long to give here.

Woodbridge, Suffolk. A Perpendicular building, probably of the latter half of the fifteenth century, in which a fine rood-screen must have taken the place of a chancel-arch, which is missing. Only the base of that screen remains. The clerestory is well lit by two windows to each bay. The seven sacraments are represented on the panels of the font

Coulsdon, Surrey. Early English sedilia and piscina

FIXTURES AND FITTINGS

THE Reformed Church did not by any means regard the vast legacy of ancient buildings they had inherited as "treasure-houses of art and historic interest" but as a considerable embarrassment. It was not only the images of saints and angels which incurred their grave displeasure but practically all the fittings and fixtures with the exception of pews and pulpit. A plain meeting-house, such as the various dissenting bodies were to build at a later time, would have suited them equally well. Nowadays, guided by archaeological considerations and a renewed sense of reverence for spiritual mysteries, feeling has run strongly in favour of preserving and repairing such things as escaped the attention of the iconoclasts, and re-exposing to view what they had attempted to conceal with masonry and whitewash.

A century of vigorous restoration (though sometimes misguided) has, in the main, been successful in recapturing much of the medieval atmosphere of our parish churches. Here is a short note on the older fittings. Among the

things built-in as part of the fabric was a stoup for holy water near the principal entrance. As half of this usually protruded it was smashed so that the remainder could be disguised with rubble and mortar and lost to memory. In the south wall of the chancel were niched seats (*sedilia*), usually three in number, for the parish priest, deacon, and sub-deacon, severally graded in elevation to accord with the dignity of their occupiers. Farther east was the piscina, a small basin under a decorated stone canopy with a drain. Into this the ablutions of the chalice were poured to pass without profanation into consecrated ground. This was concealed without difficulty, though the carving was sometimes hacked away to give a flush surface to the in-filling. The altar, a stone slab bearing its five crosses of consecration, mounted on a masonry plinth was often engaged in the stone-work of the east wall. This was invariably pulled down. But quite often the workmen seem to have hesitated to carry out the full extent of their orders to break up the

At Dunster in Somerset, the church was that of a Benedictine priory in which the vicar and townsmen had parochial rights. As often happened under such conditions there was constant friction between monks and parishioners, who finally demonstrated their grievances by removing the bell-ropes in the tower, thus dislocating the timing of the seven daily monastic services. Differences were composed in 1498 by allotting the whole of the nave to the parish, who then formed their own chancel by erecting a rood-loft across the full breadth of the building at their own expense. The loft has been dismantled but the screen (the longest in England) remains almost untouched. There is a small projection on the east side for a rood-loft altar. On the right are seen the doorways to the loft staircase

consecrated slab and, instead, to have concealed it in the earth of the churchyard or elsewhere, for many have been recovered undamaged.

There were also one or more wall cupboards (*aumbries*) whose cavities, rediscovered at some restoration, are found in the east or north walls and generally reported in guide-books. A most interesting but rarely found feature is the Easter Sepulchre, a recess, architecturally enriched, in which the consecrated elements were laid on Good Friday and removed to the altar on Easter morning, a ceremony typifying the entombment of Christ. Sometimes it was willed by a benefactor that his tomb should be placed on the north side of the chancel and have the honour of acting as this ritual repository.

The division between chancel and nave was marked not only by the arch in the party-wall but also a wooden screen (*cancellus*, whence the name) with doors. It carried a narrow gallery (*rood-loft*), on the eastern parapet of which was fixed a large crucifix (the *Holy Rood*) with the figures of the Virgin and St. John on either side, while the western parapet acted as a long candelabrum for burning wax lights (the *candle-beam*), bequests for the maintenance of which "to burn before the rood" are constantly met with in old wills. The screen and the rood had always marked this dividing line in churches from the seventh century downwards. The loft was probably an addition of the fourteenth century, to be greatly enriched and elaborated in the succeeding one, when screen and loft

South Cerney, Gloucestershire. Head of Christ, possibly from the rood

South Cerney, Gloucestershire. Head of Christ, possibly from the rood

reached their peak of magnificence. A few late examples were even carried out in stone, as at Totnes in Devonshire.

The Reformers attacked the rood-loft almost as violently as the altar though not with equal success. They made bonfires of the actual roods and their attendant figures and not a single one of these appears to have survived. But when it came to lofts and screens, whose brilliant execution in handicraft was the pride of the village, there was much resistance and evasion. Probably by perching the emblem of our earthly king, the royal arms, in the old place of honour, the screen, if not the loft, was often saved. Here was a stance at once cheap, convenient, and flattering to the new Head of the Church! At any rate a great many fine rood-screens are left, though they are rather locally distributed. Lofts are much more rare, but former access to them by doorway and stone stairs is frequently in evidence.

Barton Turf, Norfolk. Painted panels on rood-screen

In fact, the whole chancel was regarded as superfluous in a Protestant church and omitted altogether in the new ones which were built, right down to the early part of the nineteenth century. Most have had to have them added since, if only to accommodate a surpliced choir. But the Reformers took strong measures to ensure good congregations and made it a legal offence to miss attendance on Sunday, finable in the magistrate's court. This meant another enlargement of accommodation. The problem was resolved in a much cheaper way than the old one of throwing out transepts or adding aisles or new bays to the west end. It was the omnibus solution of double-decking by means of galleries, built-in with new churches and forced into the Gothic aisles of old ones. At the beginning of the present century they were still to be seen everywhere. But now they have nearly all been cleared from pre-Reformation buildings, in some cases leaving ugly scars on carved work and mouldings.

The fittings which suffered most in the nave were those of the side chapels which had been family oratories or chantries, or served craft guilds, or contained parochial altars of particular dedication. Their appurtenances were similar to those of the chancel and met with the same treatment, the restorers eventually revealing the sites of these chapels through rediscovering the tell-tale piscina in the nave wall which inevitably confirmed the position of an altar.

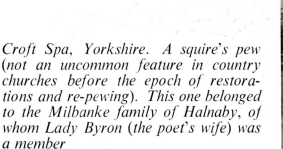

Croft Spa, Yorkshire. A squire's pew (not an uncommon feature in country churches before the epoch of restorations and re-pewing). This one belonged to the Milbanke family of Halnaby, of whom Lady Byron (the poet's wife) was a member

Croscombe, Somerset. Here, the medieval rood-screen has been replaced by a chancel-screen of contemporary Jacobean design, over which the royal arms takes the place of the figures of the rood. This, the pulpit, and woodwork of the chancel roof, were the gift of Arthur Lake, Bishop of Bath and Wells, in 1616

THE FONT

IT is the common experience to find in an old parish church a font which is at least as ancient as any of the pre-Reformation fittings, often antedating all visible parts of the fabric, a stolid twelfth-century creation, the last representative of a once all-Norman building. "Here," you may think to yourself, "is something which has stood unmoved through all the changes of men's attitude to God." Yet a very large number of these fonts (if counted it would be quite surprising) have not stood unmoved by any means but are repatriated exiles that have only returned to their old places within the last hundred and fifty years. They had been tolerated during the purges of Edward VI and Elizabeth, the Reformers of that time having merely wrenched off the hasps and staples which had secured their covers. These had formerly been padlocked to ensure that the water, with which the bowl was then kept filled and was consecrated for baptisms, was not contaminated or stolen to work charms. It was not until the Cromwellian régime that wholesale evictions were made and fonts were cast bodily out into the weather, some to the churchyard, others to the farmyard, their place taken by a plain earthenware bowl stood on a rough milking-stool. It was often as much as two centuries before they were recalled.

When a font is given a permanent canopy which is a symbolic mark of honour (something more than a font-cover) the whole can be described as a baptistry. Pre-reformation examples are rare in England. This one, at Trunch in Norfolk, can hardly be earlier than the reign of Henry VIII. The font, usually eight-sided is here hexagonal, doubtless to give more freedom of action between the pillars

It is not so easy here to draw the distinction between font-with-cover and baptistry as in the preceding, but the canopy was one of the few "superstitions" which survived the Reformation, though with confined uses and under other names. In pulpits it was called a sounding-board. The font in the picture is at Knapton in Norfolk and the canopy is dated 1704. It covers a font some 500 years older, as the arcading on the bowl indicates

Font at St. James's, Taunton, Somerset

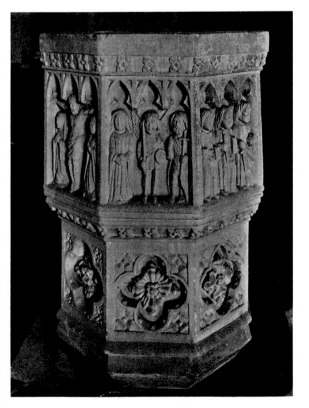

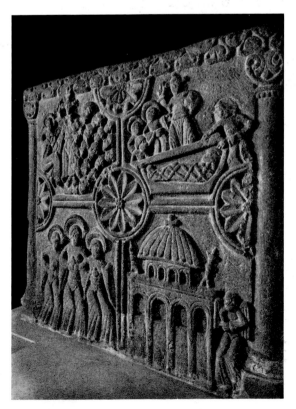

Square Norman font at Lenton, Nottinghamshire. The bottom right-hand panel is thought to be a contemporary representation of the Church of the Holy Sepulchre at Jerusalem (referred to on page 26)

73

It is quite surprising to find the number of medieval pulpits which remain, and still more so to note that the majority survived the various shocks of Reformation without the usual defacements—perhaps out of respect to the Geneva gown. Two are shown here—both from the West Country. The upper, in wood, is at Trull in Somerset, the other, in stone, at Cheddar in the same county. More monumental are those in the heart of the Midlands at Wolverhampton and Coventry which are engaged in one of the piers of the nave arcade, approached by an imposing staircase with stone balustrade. At Eddlesborough in Buckinghamshire the wooden pulpit of fifteenth century date retains its canopy of honour intact which is indistinguishable from the "sounding board" of Protestant times

THE PULPIT

T HE one piece of medieval church furniture that not only escaped criticism but was treated with profound and ever-growing respect was the pulpit. It grew not only in parochial estimation but in actual stature, culminating in the three-decker of the eighteenth century in which the parson ascended to a sort of fighting-top high enough to command the galleries as well as the interiors of the box-pews, there to launch rhetorical bolts against the common foe until released from his exertions by the fall of the last grain in the hour-glass.

Stoke d'Abernon, Surrey. Early seventeenth century pulpit imported from Flanders "but" says the Guide to the church "the backboard and sounding board of oak were added by Sir Francis Vincent in order to display his coat of arms"

The transience of life was the favourite theme expressed in church symbolism of the seventeenth and eighteenth centuries as here on the panel of the Jacobean pulpit at Stoke St. Gregory, Somerset

BENCH-ENDS

*Ancient pews at Dunsfold, Surrey, reputed to date from the
rebuilding of the church at the end of the thirteenth century*

The technique of disclosing and preserving medieval wall-paintings hidden under Puritan whitewash has made great advances within the last fifty years. St. Christopher, the patron saint of travellers very often confronted the stranger immediately on entering the church. This fourteenth century rendering is at Baunton, Gloucestershire

The space above the chancel-arch (which was large where a clerestory had been added) formed either an immediate background for the figures of the rood or a sort of sky-piece above them. Here the "doom picture" was painted, showing in vivid contrast the blissful reception of the righteous (on the right hand of the Father) and the pains of the damned on the other. This rendering at South Leigh, Oxfordshire, shows St. Michael applying the test of weighing up each soul

The carved bench-end was an art mainly developed in the West Country and East Anglia (doubtless the product of local emulation). As in the misericord, the oft-told fable was a favourite subject. Such is the story in two parts of the fox who preached to the geese and was first listened to and then found out—at Brent Knoll, Somerset

Pew panel with Renaissance "conceit", Sapperton, Gloucestershire

The gates in the Chancel-arch at Staunton Harold, Leicestershire, were erected circa *1720 and were probably designed by Robert Bakewell. The church itself was built 1653–63 during the Commonwealth. It was one of the last genuinely Perpendicular churches built in England*

Carved panel of Nottinghamshire alabast (fourteenth century) now in the north ai. of Long Melford Church. It represents t adoration of the Magi and is thought to ha been made for a reredos

Crucifix built into the wall of Daglingworth Church, Gloucestershire, with other crude carvings. Probably Saxon but very much the work of a local man

If that to Ring you doe come here,
you muſt Ring well with hand and eare.
keep ſtroak of time and goe not out;
or elſe you forfeit out of doubt.
Our law is ſo concluded here;
for every fault a jugg of beer,
if that you Ring with Spurr or Hat,
a jugg of beer muſt pay for that.
If that you take a Rope in hand;
theſe forfeits you muſt not withſtand.
or if that you a Bell ovrthrow;
it muſt coſt Six pence ere you goe.
If in this place you ſweare or curſe;
Six pence to pay pull out your purſe,
come pay the Clerk it is his fee;
for one (that ſwears) ſhall not goe free.
Theſe Laws are old, and are not new;
therefore the Clerk muſt have his due.

George Hariſon.

1694.

*Detail of glass in west window, Fairford
Church, Gloucestershire, late fifteenth century
and thought to have been made by Barnard
Flower and his glaziers who produced the glass
for King's College Chapel, Cambridge*

Tomb of Stephen Alard, a Warden of the Cinque Ports in the early fourteenth century, in Winchelsea Parish Church. The canopies of the Winchelsea tombs are among the most striking of any made in the Decorated style

Two weepers at the feet of an effigy in Strelley, Nottinghamshire; doubtless beneficiaries of deceased's charity in return for their prayers

MEMORIALS

THE memorials in an ancient church can engage us deeply in several ways. They are unique representations of historic periods and bring the past realistically before us. They touch the heart as well, being the last brave flourishes of those brief candles, of whose lights we had, till that moment, been quite ignorant. Yet we may feel somewhat drawn to them in the simple bond of having just crossed the same threshold they knew so well.

The evolution of the church monument is one of ascension and disengagement. From the eleventh to the fifteenth century, figures representing the departed, whether carved in stone or wood or outlined in the *brass*, lie prone on the floor. In the next two centuries they tend to forsake the floor for the walls where they present themselves and all members of their families in a kneeling posture. In either case their hands are folded in prayer and they look not to the right or the left. Then suddenly there is a break-away, a disengagement from horizontal or vertical backgrounds, an abandonment of formal posture. They become free statuary such as one might see in any town hall or public park. Figures and groups are not even necessarily in devotional attitudes. They may merely stand by cornucopias of hot-house fruits, or sit on an anchor, or point to a map of the world, not even sharing the grief of the winged but decidedly carnal cherubs which sit or hover near. And, even if one's Latin is not too rusty to make out those epitaphs, one has generally to read between the lines. What exhibitions of righteous pomposity! But contemptuousness would be quite out of place here, for one must reflect that those very beings of gilded memory may well be lying just below one's feet, sheeted in lead in the dark family vault, long since humbled by the sting of death.

Tomb of Margaret, Countess of Bath and her two husbands (the first reposing in the compartment below), Hengrave, Suffolk, sixteenth century

Brass at East Markham, Nottinghamshire, of Millicent, wife of Sir John Markham who arranged legal formalities for the deposition of Richard II. She died in 1419

Bronze effigy to Richard Beauchamp, Earl of Warwick (died at Rouen, 1439). The framework over the figure is a herse intended to support a velvet pall. The contract for the work, which employed many craftsmen of different kinds, still exists

Monument to Sir Henry and Dame Poole, Sapperton, Gloucestershire; early seventeenth century

Effigy of Sir Thomas Hoby (died in Paris 1566) at Bisham, Berkshire

Lady in late fifteenth-century head-dress at Clifton, Nottinghamshire

Sir Robert Atkyns, who wrote the History of Gloucestershire, seen under his hand though he died in 1711 just before publication. Sapperton, Gloucestershire

Monument to the Duchess of Montague at Warkton, Northamptonshire,
by Van Gelder in an architectural setting by Adam. She was a lady of
social importance. Her mother was the daughter of the great Duke of
Marlborough and her father the second Duke of Montague. She married
George Brudenell, 4th Earl of Cardigan, and it was somehow arranged
that on his father-in-law's death he took his wife's name and arms and
was made 1st Duke of Montague of a new creation. Thus he owed the
coronet (on the ground) to his duchess who (gestures imply) is about to
exchange it for the heavenly crown. She died in 1775. The medieval effigy
has become a group of statuary tinged with secular symbolism

Opposite: *Monument to Strode Lytton at Knebworth who died in 1710. A contemporary fashion in the buttoning of coats is faithfully reproduced*

Weston Zoyland. Essentially a tie-beam roof but of local Somerset type in which king-posts with curved braces play a part and the intervals are filled with tracery

THE ROOF

IN the Middle Ages both churches and houses (which mainly consisted of one large hall not unlike the nave of a church) were open from the floor to the rafters, and the roofing timbers offered a field for decoration. In the church the motif suggested by symbolical analogy was an obvious one: it was a sky in miniature. By filling it with angels, stars, and saints, Heaven could be brought a little nearer. But it took time to develop the convention to the full splendour it achieved at the end of the Gothic period, and, like everything else in that logical treatment of architecture, the decorative form closely followed the structural advance.

The wooden roofs of the twelfth and thirteenth centuries were simple constructions and *single-framed*. That is to say, they consisted of pairs of rafters set up fairly closely together in the interval between the stone gable-ends to support the roofing material, thatch or stone. They were fastened to each other at the apex and their feet secured to the wooden sleepers which ran along the tops of either wall (*wall-plates*). To prevent them spreading they must be tied. This was generally done by trussing them with a beam about two-thirds of the way up called a *collar*, giving each couple the appearance of a capital "A" with the stroke placed rather high. In addition, the rafters were strutted both at the collar and the foot. But each member (*truss*) remained a single individual, unconnected with its neighbour except through the common attachment to the wall-plate. This variety of single-framing, called the *trussed rafter* roof, seems to have been the most general until the fourteenth century. Its main drawback was that individual members tended to spread and cause distortion to the whole roof, exerting an outward thrust on the walls which would then bulge outwards in spite of external buttressing.

To check this dangerous tendency the medieval carpenter devised the *double-framed* system. In this a much more substantial truss was introduced at intervals, each linked securely to the other by longitudinal beams called *purlins* which ran along either slope of the roof, and also with a continuous *ridge-piece* at the apex. The purlins and the ridge were fastened above these principal rafters, while the common rafters were borne on top of them. Over a limited span, a roof of this kind was sufficiently rigid to rest on the walls with a downward pressure only and no outward thrust, like the

lid on a box. But several new tendencies were at work. One was to pay more attention to the aesthetic possibilities of the roof, now that the larger windows with their traceried heads admitted so much more light into the body of the church—and double-framing actually invited this treatment. Another was the desire for greater width in new and reconstructed naves and also the addition to them of clerestories.

All these considerations increased the danger of spreading but only the first will need any explanation. The thing which rather marred the good looks of a roof was that A-like bar, the collar. It would be so much better to reduce its size by placing it higher up in the peak or getting rid of it altogether. In either case the structural check on spreading would be weakened. The carpenters gained their end, however, by quite a simple but most effective invention—the *wall-post*. This was a stout

The Barn Chapel at Bures, Suffolk. A thirteenth-century trussed rafter roof; originally single-framed, but purlins introduced later for strengthening

Lympsham, Somerset. This type of roof, found throughout the West Country and used down to the sixteenth century, is an adaptation of the trussed rafter type with curved struts and braces. It is divided into squares by cross-batons of no structural value and the intervening spaces filled in with lath-and-plaster. At Shepton Mallet (page 70) the spaces are filled with carved panels. The great feature is the display of carved bosses for which the criss-cross gives an opportunity

vertical post attached to the foot of each principal rafter. It descended several feet down the inner face of the wall to a bracket. Two purposes in anti-spread were then served at once. The whole structure was thereby definitely anchored within the walls (a great relief to the wall-plates) and the outward thrust, instead of impinging altogether at the point of junction, was distributed along these posts to a lower point.

The first-fruits of this invention is seen in the

arch-braced roof which practically eliminated the collar. It made its appearance before the middle of the fourteenth century and sorted poetically with the Decorated style of the building which it crowned.

But that was not the end of what the wall-post could do. It proceeded to father yet another improvement at the beginning of the fifteenth century which became the last great glory of the Gothic roof and caused the parish church with its woodwork to rival in splendour the great stone vaults of cathedrals and monastic churches. This was the *hammer-beam* —a beam projected horizontally from the top of the wall-post, braced to the foot of it by a curved piece, the whole shape of the member like that of the iron bracket one uses when putting up a shelf. Again, from the end of the hammer-beam another vertical post ascended to the slope of the rafter so that the whole had something of the effect of a lattice-girder. This

last structural improvement gave the wood-carver his greatest moment. On the ends of the hammer-beams he could now poise angels with spread wings which actually floated in mid-air above the worshippers, while the wall-posts gave a new range of niches for saints in glory.

Those two principles of arch-brace and hammer-beam, though built severally, were often most effectively combined in the empyrean

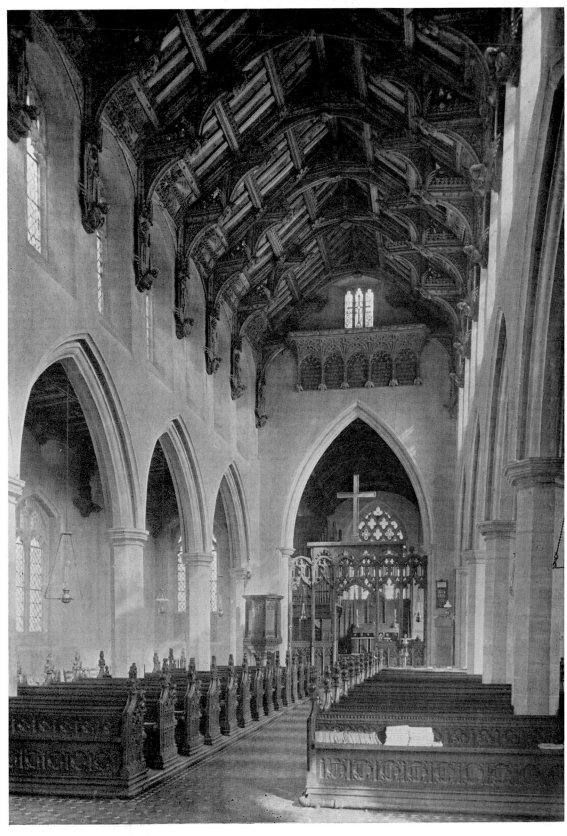

Woolpit, Suffolk. Double hammer-beam roof with angels hovering at the ends of the hammer-beams and the brackets from which the wall-posts spring. The wall-posts themselves are niched for saints. Above the chancel-arch is a coved canopy which once did honour to the now vanished figures of the rood

North Cerney, Gloucestershire. A cambered tie-beam roof of fifteenth century type though with rather more pitch than usual. The stone pulpit is pre-Reformation

of the high-pitched roof. But this time-honoured form was already being outmoded by the middle of the fifteenth century in favour of the nearly flat roof covered by lead instead of tiles, stone slates, or thatch. The support for this type of covering required much less carpentry and though adapted forms of the older kinds were retained in places, little more than simple cambered beams were really necessary as principals, and enrichments took mainly the more formal shape of carved bosses at the intersection of common rafters and purlins and along the main beams.

Plaster ceilings in both churches and houses were unknown before the days of the Tudors. They began in houses which, for the first time, received upper floors. When church building started again a century after the Reformation the lath-and-plaster ceiling had become so firmly established as "the thing to have" that it was not only installed in the new church, where it naturally harmonised with Renaissance design, but contrived in most of the old ones, for open-timber roofs, no matter how richly embellished, were now regarded as completely *démodé*. In the new churches the ceilings were generally coffered and moulded and given a good deal of floral ornament in plaster, but the rectified transformations in the Gothic buildings were too flimsy in structure to stand such weight. Some, however, were relieved by painting and given an exceedingly crude version of the heavenly host, surging in and out of black clouds, blowing toy trumpets.

But now nearly all the plain ceilings in the old churches have met the same deserts as the galleries and box pews and have been removed to reveal once more the carpentry and carving of the Middle Ages; a few painted ones having been preserved on archaeological grounds.

We are fortunate in being the immediate heirs to an age which returned to a love of its old parish churches and was wealthy enough to pay for restorations which, in the main, were well and sympathetically directed. We should make the most of what we have, for decay is setting in again. The State is spending far more money on the upkeep of ruins than on these buildings of a still enduring spiritual use and the next age may not have the means to prevent their gradual collapse.

Cirencester, Gloucestershire. Fan-vaulting in St. Katharine's Chapel at the parish church, completed 1530

Church clock with striking Jacks of Tudor date at St. Mary-Steps, Exeter. The central figure is called Matthew the Miller and is believed to be intended for Henry VIII

INDEX

INDEX